A GLIMPSE INTO MY LIFE

SYLVIE FEGHALI SMITH

A
Glimpse
into my
Life

A Collection of Micro-Memoirs

SPRING CEDARS

A Glimpse into my Life is a work of creative nonfiction. Some names and identifying details have been changed.

Copyright © 2019 by Sylvie Feghali Smith

Printed in the United States of America.
First edition, 2019

Book cover, design, and editing by Spring Cedars

ISBN 978-1-950484-02-7 (paperback)
ISBN 978-1-950484-03-4 (ebook)

Published by Spring Cedars LLC
Centennial, Colorado
info@springcedars.com

Foreword

A Glimpse into my Life is a collection of micro-memoirs by Sylvie Feghali Smith, originally composed and presented as speeches in the period of 2004 to 2007.

Sylvie immigrated to the United States with her family in 1983. She began a new life in Columbia, South Carolina, adapting to American culture and the English language along the way. It was in this interest that she became a charter member of the IST Power Rangers Toastmasters, a public speaking club. As a number of severe personal trials tested her resolve—being laid off, a chaotic divorce, and the untimely passing of her beloved father—Sylvie used the Toastmasters club as a means of expressing and exploring the events that would eventually shape the geography of her life.

Sylvie's accomplishments in Toastmasters are noteworthy. The speeches included in this collection were selected for *Best Speaker* every time a vote was taken. Sylvie won the International Speech Area Contest with *The Road Least Traveled*. She also took home her club's inaugural *Speaker of the Year* award. After delivering twenty speeches, she retired with the rank of *Advanced Communicator Bronze*.

Upon hearing or reading Sylvie's speeches, fellow toastmasters, family, and friends urged her to publish them as short stories. Several years later she decided to compile her favorites into a book.

Her story, through trial, tribulation, and sometimes intense personal emotion, is a sincere illustration of resiliency and passion from the perspective of an immigrant single mother. Sylvie's determined spirit and the inspiration she draws from her family's sacrifice and faith, consistently ring throughout the speeches. These motifs offer four crucial themes: Hidden behind darkness, there remains a light. In every hardship, there is perseverance. A heart that loves will be remembered. When you fall, you bounce back.

Each story in this collection explores a smaller piece of the greater whole that is Sylvie's life. In a few anecdotes, the author presents a series of significant personal moments through humor and self-reflection. Though first composed as speeches, the messages retain the same sincerity as the day they were delivered. Whether through her struggles, revelations, or simple wit, Sylvie manages to express her entire world. You are invited to take a glimpse into the window of her life.

Daniel James Haddad
Columbia, SC
November 2019

Can you guess where I was born?

April 4, 2000

Ladies and gentlemen,

I would like to introduce you to myself.

I was born in a small country on the eastern shores of the Mediterranean Sea.

Unlike its neighbors, it has no desert, no oil.

Unlike its neighbors, it has two chains of mountains separated by a fertile valley, the Bekaa Valley.

It has the highest peaks in the area, with crowded ski slopes and numerous beach resorts.

It houses over five hundred prehistoric temples dating back to thousands of years before Christ.

Its name was first mentioned in tablets from 2900 BC as well as in notable literature, including the Bible.

It is the country where Jesus performed his first miracle.

Can you guess where I was born?

Growing up, I was never able to visit the town where Jesus transformed water into wine. In fact, I only visited two of the five hundred temples scattered throughout the land. I am a Christian, and that area was Muslim territory, which was forbidden to us.

I learned a lot of lessons in my teenage years.

I learned about fighting, kidnapping, hate, revenge, death, rations of food and electricity. I remember sleepless nights spent on the ground floor along with the other neighbors. We lived at the top of the building, and a 155-mm bomb could go through one or even two floors. Everybody systematically migrated downstairs. We played backgammon and cards. Guessing whether the explosion we just heard originated from a canon that was firing away from a nearby station, or if it was one heading in our direction.

I remember waking up every morning and wondering if we had school that day. No, I was not considering the possibility of a snow day or a hurricane threat. It was just an ordinary morning in my country in the late seventies and early eighties.

I remember studying for hours to the light of a candle for an exam that would not take place, as school would close because of nearby bombings or damages from the previous night.

I remember April 2nd, 1980. We were taking a math test when the blasting started at a rate never witnessed before. As the explosions grew close, the students raised their heads and stared at the teacher. I remember his words, "Ladies, you have twenty minutes left if we stay alive ..."

As I stand before you today, many years have gone by. I am now the mother of two boys. When my children ask about my country, I try to share the good memories.

I tell them about playing in the forest with my cousins, climbing to the top of the olive trees, pretending that they were airplanes transporting us to faraway places.

I tell them about eating grapes straight from the vine and fresh figs from the tree.

I tell them about collecting wild flowers in the spring.

I tell them about dyeing Easter eggs with onion peels, dried herbs and florets, and about the egg breaking contests at the dawn of Easter.

I tell them about picking oregano in the woods, letting it dry through the summer, then mixing it with olive oil, salt, and sumac to prepare the best tasting breakfast.

I tell them about Sunday afternoon drives to the airport where my dad would treat us to ice cream. It was delicious, that cold sweetness melting on my tongue.

I tell them about yearly pilgrimages to the mimosa trees on Mother's Day, where we arranged the largest flowers into a beautiful bouquet for my mom.

I tell them about fall mornings, when it was crisp from the night's rain. We bundled up and headed to the woods to collect escargots as they came out of hibernation, and competed to find the biggest one. To this day, my cousin Joumana still claims she regularly won, but we all know that's far from the truth.

I tell them about building snowmen and sliding down the mountain on a winter day, then heading down to the coast for a swim.

I tell them about the most majestic experience in the world. Imagine floating in the warm Mediterranean waters under a sunny blue sky. Glorious mountains face you, on top of which stands the statue of Mary, Mother of Jesus. Presiding over a shrine built for her by the faithful, she smiles and extends her arms toward the Bay of Jounieh to welcome you.

When Daniel and Michael think about where their mother grew up, I hope they hold on to these positive images and feelings.

Ladies and gentlemen, I hope that you, too, will conjure up these pretty pictures the next time you hear or read about my country.

I was born in Lebanon.

Sylvie Feghali Smith, Michael Haddad, and Daniel
Haddad in Baalbek, Lebanon. 2009. Author's personal
collection.

We are moving where?

July 30, 2004

"Columbia, South Carolina," my father declared.

"Where? Never heard of it. Doesn't matter anyway. I'm not going."

"We all go or nobody goes," my father replied in a sad but firm tone.

The year was 1983, in Bsous, a small mountain town fifteen minutes east of Beirut. It was a hot, dry day, as Mediterranean summers tend to be.

My dad was visiting. During these happy moments, we went on numerous family outings. My father had been working on industrial construction projects in the Arab countries and Africa since 1975. He would live abroad for four months, then spend three to four weeks back home with us. This was a typical way of life for Lebanese fathers, for the war had deteriorated the nation's economy.

This visit, however, was different. My father disclosed that he was suffering from a chronic disease. His kidneys were at ten percent capacity and would stop functioning in the near future. Doctors had strictly forbidden him to work in remote areas, which meant my family would no longer have a source of income. Major crisis.

At eighteen I was the oldest, then came my three brothers who were seventeen, thirteen, and ten. My mother was a homemaker. None of us had ever worked for money, and it was impossible to find a job in such a war-torn country.

This was the first time I had seen my mother, the strongest person I knew, cry. She always held her chin up high and took care of us single-handedly while dad worked abroad. During the war, she shuttled the four of us from town to town, away from bullets and missiles. My mother did everything to protect us, even when she had kidney stones. With an

IV bag in one hand and my youngest brother in the other, she would sleep with us in the hallway where the attic provided an additional shield from dropping bombs.

This time, she did not have to dodge gunfires and explosions. It was a much stronger force, one we call our destiny.

My maternal uncle suggested we move to the United States. My mother could find a job there, he said. My brothers and I would go to college and work at the same time. Dad would receive treatment. There was no other option. "If you stay," he told my parents, "the children will have no future."

Life was not fair. I had just turned eighteen and passed the official exams of Math Elementary with flying colors. I had taken the entrance examination to the Lebanese University College of Engineering, where they accepted the top two hundred of two thousand applicants. I had cut out the article from the newspaper where "Sylvie Feghali" was typed. My future was just starting. I had big dreams.

I hated destiny. I thought God created us free to make our own destiny. Catholicism was so confusing. How could we be free and destined at the same time? I was not going to the United States, my future was here. They could go if they wanted.

"We all go or nobody goes," my dad's words resonated in my mind.

What choice did I have, after all? What would I do if I stayed behind? I couldn't even drive. Being alone at eighteen in a war-torn country, when you have no money, when you cannot drive. The circumstances were not ideal.

It was only a matter of weeks before we piled six people and twelve suitcases in my cousin's car, and headed toward that destiny of ours. Since the airport was shut down, we had to board a ship to Larnaca, Cyprus.

From there, we would fly to the United States. As the ship pulled away from shore and floated further into the Mediterranean, the sound of explosions faded away. The sight of my country became smaller as my tears grew bigger.

"You will never come back," my physics teacher had told me.

I promised myself I would find him.

After a forty-hour adventure across the Atlantic Ocean, worthy of its own narrative, we landed at LaGuardia airport in New York City. At customs, a blond man with blue eyes stood tall. It was 3:00 am. He did not seem very excited to see six people and twelve suitcases at that hour. Especially when he realized he had to take our photographs for the Green Card application. It was Saturday, September 16th, 1983. He asked if we were carrying alcohol.

"All my children!" my mother answered in her best English.

He stared at her, at our tattered suitcases, then back at our tired but proud and honest faces. The officer shook his head and said, "Welcome to the United States."

We completed the formalities and were transported to a hotel for the night before taking a plane to our final destination. The hotel looked like it had jumped out of a movie screen, so high and so clean. Best of all, no bullet holes and no tape on the windows. In the room, I turned on the TV and was taken aback. It was all in English. No subtitles! I flipped through a few more channels before it hit me: I would have to learn English.

The following day, we landed in Columbia, South Carolina, and after spending the first month crying and refusing to leave the house, I eventually wandered outside to discover my new world.

Columbia, South Carolina.
Population: 124,732.

53 percent female, 47 percent male.

Median Age: 35.5

Major Attractions: The Koger Center of the Art, Riverbanks Zoo, the State Museum.

Major Educational Centers: The University of South Carolina.

That's what research told me.

The data I have gathered in person throughout the years is more compelling. Columbia is the hospitable city that welcomed my family over twenty years ago. It is where my mother went to work, and my dad stayed home and learned how to cook. It is where my mother learned enough English to realize that "all my children" would have been the right answer, if the customs officer had asked why we were immigrating to the United States.

"We all come or nobody does," my father had said. It was for our future that my parents decided to emigrate.

Columbia is where my father struggled for

his life, where he died in December 2003, and where he is buried. It is where my parents, who never completed high school, proudly celebrated the college graduation of their four children from the University of South Carolina.

It is where my father taught me how to drive, where he bought my first car. It is where I got my first job as an engineer at NCR. It is where I fell in love, married, later divorced. It is where I had my first child, as well as my second. Where I learned that soccer is not football, and that "Southern" is the official language in South Carolina, not English. It is where I became infatuated with sweet iced tea and fried okra.

Through the ups and downs, this city is where I spent most of my life. Although I may never be a southern belle, or crave a barbecue sandwich, or be able to say y'all with the right accent, Columbia, South Carolina, is the place that I call home.

Olan Mills. Photograph of Chad Feghali, Sylvie Feghali Smith, Bechara Feghali, Frank Feghali, Samia Feghali, and Fadi Feghali in Columbia, South Carolina. 1985. Copyright by Lifetouch.

A Red Rose and Chocolate-Covered Strawberries

October 12, 2004

It was a glorious spring day in Columbia, South Carolina, gorgeous weather, blooming azaleas and beautiful blue skies. The waterfall at Finlay Park never looked prettier, the sun was hitting it just at the right spot, creating a cascade of sparkles.

It was 7:30 am. I parked at the bottom of the hill and eased my way to the top. It was already very crowded. As I searched for my running team, a multi-colored sea of spandex shorts and cropped tops engulfed me. What was I doing here? The bodies swirling around me were lean and muscular. It was obvious I did not belong. Was I going to make it through this race? Why had I gotten myself into this to begin with?

It had almost been a month earlier when Laurie, the running club captain at my church, asked if I would run a race.

"You must be joking. I am no runner. I sometimes jog, but only so I can eat more."

"Certainly, you can do it," she encouraged. "Besides, we need a fifth person to get the discount."

I promised to think about it.

She had caught me at one of the most insane and arduous times of my life. I had lost my fourteen-year old job due to the closing of NCR Teradata, and for four months, almost went crazy hunting for a new position. This was when I started to run not just for exercise, but because it became an obsession. I needed a job, so running became my job.

It was during these morning runs that I made up my mind about my marriage. My family had generously shared their unsolicited evaluations of my marital situation, but I had to come to my own conclusion. Eventually, I filed for separation and was now dealing with its effects on my life and that of my two sons.

Then, my father became extremely ill. He spent most of the year in hospitals. Doctors were unable to diagnose the condition. Every evening, my children and I went to visit him. While I was diving straight into the overwhelming tunnel of single motherhood, I still painted a smile on my face to keep my fathers' spirits up.

A running race? Why not? Something for me. A challenge! I loved challenges.

I completed the registration, and there I was, Race Day, May 17th, 2003, just a few minutes from the start. I found Laurie and the others. At least we had the wits to participate in an all-women's race. No need to make a spectacle in front of a bunch of men.

The contestants were hustling and bustling. We were instructed to pick up our chip, a device that would track our individual speed, and attach it to our shoelaces. The timer would begin when crossing the start line and stop when passing the finish line. The next piece of gear to collect was a bib which displayed our number. I proudly pinned 1079 on my race shirt.

Then, an epiphany. I was transformed into a professional runner. "Ladies clear the way, number 1079 is here to set a new world record." I scanned the crowd, but nobody else seemed to think much of my solemn moment. A dozen women had already started running. In my highly experienced athlete's mind, I found them foolish. One would want to preserve energy before a race, right?

"They are warming up," Laurie explained.

"I thought that's what the first mile was for." The laughter following my comment was interrupted with a loud announcement. The time had come.

Two hundred thirty-six fierce women assembled at the start line. A short speech was given and, then, a gun fired. Or maybe it was my imagination. Everyone began to run, and at first I felt a bit claustrophobic. But the sprinters advanced quickly and, much to my relief, created a welcomed clearance.

The track was beautiful, taking us through the winding streets of downtown Columbia. My heart beat faster and faster as I increased my strides. Yet, I was not tired. I was running my first race. Who would have thought.

A team of cheerleaders was positioned on the corner of Assembly and Lady Street. They were clapping and shouting words of encouragement. It was inspiring. My eyes filled with tears. I was overwhelmed by all the people standing on the sidelines, applauding and motivating. They supported us from the bottom of their hearts, and it was unbelievable.

My intention for the race was to keep up with the nine-minute per mile pacer, but she was nowhere to be seen. At that point, Laurie zoomed by, and I asked about the nine-minute pacer. She suggested we try to find her. "You go right ahead," I replied. I had never experienced this many people cheering me on with such energy. Now, I intended to savor every minute.

The first two miles were effortless, I was so excited and barely noticed the slope up Gervais Street. The huffing and puffing kicked in soon enough, and the thought of stopping crossed my mind. But I could not let my new fans down.

The fourth mile was more manageable, and I was able to catch my breath on the last downhill segment of the race.

You should have seen me cross that finish line. I felt like a celebrity. Number 1079 was displayed on the big screen, and I was handed a beautiful red rose, my Olympic medal!

Ladies, if you ever decide to run a race, The Providence Heart & Sole Women's Five Miler is the one. The post-race festivities included, in addition to the red rose, a scrumptious breakfast complete with pineapple cream cheese bagels, succulent chocolate-dipped strawberries (my favorites), an assortment of cakes, breakfast sandwiches, fruits …

The moment I returned home, I rushed to my computer and sent everyone I knew an email announcing that I, Sylvie, ran my first race and placed in the top fifty percent. Okay, okay, so I was ranked one hundred seventeen out of two hundred thirty-six. But I was faster than more than half the runners!

Imagine the surprise. My cousin Aline replied from Lebanon, "What do you mean you ran a race? Women in our family don't race! That is a known fact."

My liberal cousin Tony emailed, "What are you doing racing? You should be at home, barefoot, cooking and cleaning, and not to forget, pregnant."

My father was new to the concept of racing. He wanted to know if I had won. I told him, of course, I completed the race. He said, "yes, yes I know you completed the race, but did you win?" I explained that my objective was to finish the race not to finish it first. He did not seem very impressed. As far as he was concerned, there was too much hoopla and no medal to show.

I was in a euphoric state and neither my father's reaction, nor my cousin Tony's image of the perfect Mediterranean woman, could bring me down. My thirty-eight-year-old body ran a five-mile race in forty-seven minutes and twelve seconds. I felt so fulfilled.

In terms of calories, I must have consumed more at that post-race breakfast than I had lost during the entire race. But it was well worth it, I had a story to share with my grandchildren. But more importantly, I had received the most stunning red rose and the most scrumptious chocolate-covered strawberries. It sure beat my last few Valentines.

Sylvie Feghali Smith at The Providence Heart & Sole
Women's Five Miler in Columbia, South Carolina. 2003.
Author's personal collection.

A Pinewood Derby Memory

February 11, 2005

"Next Saturday is the big race."

"A race? What kind of race?"

"The Pinewood Derby."

"What exactly is that?"

"Oh, this must be your first year in cub scouting."

Indeed, it was. I had enrolled Daniel so we could build meaningful scouting memories together.

The Pinewood Derby was the most exciting event in cub scouting. "Each participant designs and builds a car, then we race them. It's a lot of fun," the Scout Master explained.

Build a car? Thoughts of past car building experiences flashed through my mind. I was a senior at the University of South Carolina. The Institute of Electrical and Electronic Engineers sponsored a yearly car race at their

Southeastern conference. One year, their specifications required a self-powered, self-directed car, that is, one smart enough to "feel its way" around the track without hitting the walls. I had designed state machines and was invited to join the design team. This was where I discovered that theory and reality do not always go hand in hand. Luckily, the project was optional, and I resigned, claiming I had car-building-phobia.

Yes, I was an engineer. I graduated magna cum laude from the College of Electrical Engineering and even went back for a master's degree, but that did not mean I could actually build devices. When meeting people, they often assumed I could fix their electronic equipment. I dated a man who once asked if I could repair his antique lamp. I advised him to date an electrician.

The Scout Master dropped into my hands a block of wood, four pins, and four wheels, snapping me out of my daydreaming. We were to turn these inanimate objects into a mean racing machine?

"Don't worry, we are holding a workshop to help you."

Daniel and I arrived early to the workshop. Several fathers were already busy crafting or boasting about previous experiences. I listened while my eyes focused on our piece of wooden block. I wished for a magic wand and even tried "abracadabra" in a futile attempt to escape the ordeal.

But no, my car-building-phobia had to be conquered. So what if I was the only unhandy mother in this sea of crafty fathers? After all, I was an engineer, right? Energized with new found enthusiasm, we whipped up a design that my technical brain deemed most aerodynamic. I even convinced Daniel that we were about to make Derby history.

We took our blueprint to the carpenter and watched in amazement as our first Pinewood Derby car came to life. It was a memorable moment.

The seasoned Cub Scout fathers were eager to offer their expert advice. They informed us that we needed to carve the bottom of the car and glue a weight, which had to yield a total of no more than five ounces. The weight had to fit nicely inside the car's body, without sticking out, or we could risk disqualification. They warned of the possibility of wheels falling off during the race and suggested adding a small dot of glue to ensure that the pins stuck to the wood.

No big deal, we had this. I bought weights, spray paint, and sand paper. I didn't own any carving tools, so we used a Swiss army knife I had bought in Switzerland a few years back. An hour later, I realized that carving wood with a Swiss army knife was not an easy undertaking. My arm was severely aching, and I had to take an Advil, then go to rest in bed.

The following day, I tried my best to ignore

the pain in my arm and continued building. We sanded the car, glued the weight, applied several coats of gold paint, attached the wheels, and added a drop of glue to the pins. My excitement increased as our project came together. Daniel was bubbling.

Saturday morning, as I examined the car in a last-minute inspection, I realized with horror that we had inadvertently glued the wheels to the wood. As such, the wheels refused to turn. They were sealed, stuck, super glued.

Daniel's eyes filled with tears. My arm was throbbing. My brain was hurting. And my self-esteem … That engineering degree really came in handy this time.

Frantic, I yanked on the pins, only to realize that the super glue had met its quality assurance claim. I changed strategies and pulled on the wheels. Alleluia, they came off. But a closer look revealed that they had not come off alone. The entire wooden wheel arch panel also broke off. Wonderful! How were we going to stick the pins back on? We had forty-five minutes before the race, and Daniel and I were not about to declare defeat.

I called my father. "Do you have any duct tape?" He was surprised. I had always expressed interest in books, shoes, clothes, but never duct tape. "Just have it out and ready, please. We're coming over."

We sprinted to my parents' home. Dad was waiting at the door, duct tape in hand. He shook his head as I taped the wood, the pins, and the wheels to the bottom of the golden car.

The judges, probably finding the duct tape to be a clever aesthetic touch, qualified the car to race. I was happy to report that our little golden car rolled down the race track and successfully reached the finish line, albeit several seconds after its competitors.

A week after the race, I had to seek medical attention for my arm, which I was unable to lift due to the excruciating pain. It took several months of anti-inflammatory medication and muscle relaxers, until I was prescribed therapy. My little Swiss Army knife carving exercise had inflamed my rotator cuff muscle, and it took another six months before the soreness subsided. Just in time for ... you guessed it, the next Pinewood Derby. I had created enough memories around this race the first go-around to last me a lifetime.

So I leave you with a word of Derby advice:

If you decide to help that special little one in your life to build a winning Pinewood Derby car, don't call me. I'm just an engineer.

Daniel Haddad at The Pinewood Derby in Columbia,
South Carolina. 2001. Author's personal collection.

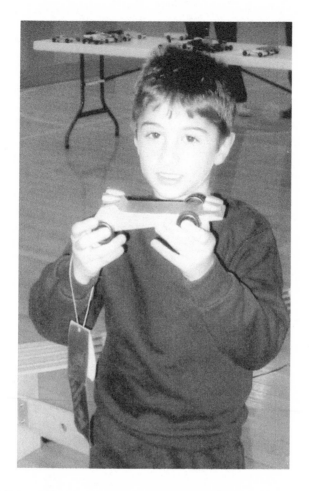

Michael Haddad at The Pinewood Derby in Columbia, South Carolina. 2003. Author's personal collection.

Sylvie Feghali Smith and her sons went on to survive many more races. Michael Haddad became an Eagle Scout.

The Road Least Traveled

December 17, 2004

"Sylvie, your son's IQ is 126. He is the smartest child in school. However, without medication, he will not perform at his IQ level. He has ADHD."

"ADHD?"

"It is common in male children. But with this medicine, he will do just fine. It has been used since the sixties and works very well."

"Doctor, can you give my son medication that would make him say 'yes ma'am?'"

"Sylvie, you know I can't do that, but I assure you, I have examined him thoroughly, and he has Attention-Deficit Hyperactivity Disorder."

ADHD, the dreadful acronym that has become an essential component of the American household.

What is it? What causes it? How is it diagnosed?   How is it treated? Are people who have it really sick? Is our technologically advanced society drugging children as a substitute to managing their behavior?

What is ADHD?

The United States Center of Disease Control defines it as:

"A disruptive behavior disorder characterized by on-going inattention and/or hyperactivity-impulsivity occurring in several settings and more frequently and severely than is typical for individuals in the same stage of development. Symptoms begin before age 7 years and can cause serious difficulties in home, school or work life."

What causes ADHD?

The most accepted theory labels the condition as a neurobiological disorder. The frontal lobes of our brain allow us to solve problems, plan ahead, understand the behavior of others, and restrain our impulses. Researchers believe that the white matter in the brain, which serves to connect the different brain regions, is smaller in children with ADHD.

How is ADHD diagnosed?

There is no lab test or psychological test that can confirm or deny ADHD. Yet, one-tenth to one-fourth of American children have been diagnosed, at a growth rate of four hundred percent since 1988. Diagnosis is based on checklists, as well as interviews with parents, teachers, and primary care-givers. It is subjective and can be abused easily. I am horrified at the number of children being diagnosed by urgent care clinics, often within a single consultation. Some, like my son, have gone through a dozen visits to the psychologist, piles of paperwork, and over one thousand dollars in fees.

How is it treated?

There are three treatment options: behavioral management, chemical management, and a combination of the two. Behavioral management is the road least traveled. It is long, requiring a great deal of patience and constancy. Chemical management is the most popular alternative. An array of stimulant prescriptions such as Ritalin, Concerta, Aderrall, Dexedrine, and Metadate, is administered. These medications contain methylphenidate, amphetamine, or dextroamphetamine as active drugs. Research shows that methylphenidate increases the release of dopamine, a neurotransmitter that appears in the brain as that white matter I referred to earlier. This drug, therefore, improves attention and focus in individuals who have weaker dopamine signals and little white matter in the brain.

Daniel's doctor prescribed Metadate. The

idea of putting my son on a medication that would affect his central nervous system was alarming. Yes, I am every pediatrician's nightmare parent. I googled ADHD and came across more than five million results. A quick search of Attention Deficit Disorder yielded nearly four hundred thousand pages. I had plenty of information to draw from and discovered that the medications used are Schedule II drugs. This outraged me. The Texas State board of Pharmacy defines Schedule II drugs as:

"Drugs with a high abuse risk, but also have safe and accepted medical uses in the United States. These drugs can cause severe psychological or physical dependence. Schedule II drugs include certain narcotic, stimulant, and depressant drugs. Some examples are morphine, cocaine, oxycodone (Percodan®), methylphenidate (Ritalin®), and dextroamphetamine (Dexedrine®)."

This must be some kind of gross mistake.

What to do?

I did more research. Unfortunately, there is no consensus within the medical field itself, with some professionals arguing that ADHD is not even a disease. They are skeptical of its widespread diagnosis and appalled at the number of children being coerced into taking Schedule II medications.

For days, I forgot how to sleep. When I did, I was in a terrorizing nightmare, where out of the darkness, vampires from pharmaceutical companies preyed on my son.

Daniel was scoring one hundred percent on tests and zeros on homework. He just did not do it, and as a result, his overall GPA suffered. So I looked into Metadate and found that, besides being a narcotic, it had serious additional side effects, including insomnia, irritability, stunted growth, heart palpitations, cardiac arrhythmia to name a few. Was getting a higher GPA worth all these risks?

Enraged, I called the doctor who assured me that when taken at the prescribed dosage, methylphenidate was perfectly safe and non-addictive. I ended up purchasing the Metadate. Who was I to question a medical professional?

The following morning, while taking a pill out of the package for Daniel, I froze. How could I tell my son that drugs are bad and at the same time hand him a Schedule II pill? I could not do it.

By now, Daniel was convinced he had a disease. He came home one evening and said, "Mom, can you please give me a pill so I can do my homework?"

It felt like a bomb fell on my head. I grabbed pencil and paper, handed them to Daniel, and said, "Son, this is all you need to do your homework. There is no Easter Bunny, there is no Tooth Fairy, and there is no Magic Homework Pill." I took the

Metadate and threw it all in the trash.

How did we get to this point?

In his book *Ritalin is Not the Answer*, Dr. David Stein changes the term from ADHD to "Inattentive and Highly Misbehaving (IA and HM)." How does this alternate label affect your perception of the problem? Daniel prefers the acronym BISS, "Bored in School Syndrome." Regardless of the name, I am convinced that my son exhibits all symptoms, including defiance, disorganization, time mismanagement, impulsivity, difficulty switching tasks, easily distracted, and detail forgetfulness. However, I am unconvinced that the solution comes in the form of a narcotic pill. I concur with Dr. Stein, "if you teach children drug taking, they will learn taking drugs."

In *Care of the Soul*, author Thomas Moore describes our technologically based lifestyle as the "Modernist Syndrome." Our society has become fixated on instant gratification: fast food, drive-through banking, emails. We have come to expect instant remedy to our ailments. We are too busy and unable to wait.

Our society lives under a great deal of stress. Most families have two working parents, some a single working parent. We barely spend any quality time with our children, our evenings are overloaded with extra-curricular activities, meal preparations, homework, baths, and clean-ups. Dr. Stein explains how these parental stresses have negative impacts on children. His recommendation is a back to the basics approach to parenting and teaching. In other words, behavioral management.

Daniel is currently enrolled in the Challenging Horizons program offered by the University of South Carolina School of Psychology at Hand Middle School. It is designed to help children with attention problems through behavioral modifications.

No drugs are involved.

The Conclusion?

Let me clarify, I do not dismiss the existence of severe ADHD cases, which do require medication. I simply do not believe those to be the majority.

We bring our children into this world. In doing so, we owe them time, love, and nurturing. They need us to be their advocates. Don't rush into popular and seemingly easy solutions, do your research, make informed decisions. In the end, you know what is right for your child, better than any pediatrician, psychologist, or neurologist. Your knowledge may not come from textbooks or with a certification, but trust that it has been bestowed upon you by a much greater power. Trust your parental instincts. Mine led me to the road least traveled. Where will yours lead you?

Daniel Haddad and Michael Haddad in Columbia, South Carolina. 2002. Author's personal collection.

Daniel Haddad graduated from the University of South Carolina with a BA in International Studies, and Michael Haddad graduated with a BS in Mechanical Engineering from the University of South Carolina.

A Tribute to Teta Camilia

August 8, 2005

My grandmother lived her life, and she lived it with passion. Not a passion for material things, it was something much greater. She dedicated her life to one goal: paying homage to her creator.

She was a loyal wife to my grandfather, who shared and perhaps exceeded her religious convictions. Together, they raised a family of eight, through life's many tribulations. They endured the Second World War, withstood instabilities in Lebanon before and during the civil war, immigrated to the United States, and dealt with starting a new chapter in a foreign country. The key to their survival? Rock-solid faith.

Teta Camilia was a fervent Catholic believer. Not a day went by without her attending Mass or praying the Rosary. I remember watching her one evening. It is the most vivid memory I have of her, a distinct image, forever etched in my mind. She sat on a chair, no longer able to kneel, and faced the statue of Mary, which had a candle lit on both sides. Teta Camilia held the rosary and twirled her fingers through the beads as each "Hail Mary" came to a close. Her expression was filled with emotion and certainty. Her eyes teared up as the words jumped from her heart through her lips, and her fingers trembled as she made the sign of the cross.

While observing, I felt touched, humbled, and somewhat ashamed at my own convictions, which paled in comparison. Teta Camilia's passion and faith were so strong they could turn an atheist into a believer.

As a child, I remember visiting my grandparents on weekends. My mother would go to great lengths to bake a delicious multi-layered cake. It was too big for any of our containers, so she wrapped it in aluminum foil and held on to it with great care, all the way from Beirut to Hazmieh. When we arrived, my three brothers and I would immediately devour the entire cake, and my grandmother was left with a big mess to clean up. I can still hear her voice as she addressed my mother on our way out, "Daughter, the cake was very nice. Thank you. Next time, it may be easier to feed it to your kids at home, and then come over to visit."

Anyone who met Teta Camilia undoubtedly thinks of her laughter. It resonated true joy, a joy that could only be achieved by someone in complete peace with the external and internal worlds. She welcomed visitors with this unforgettable laughter, even when she was not up for company. She was without exception, a hospitable and generous hostess.

Her home was adorned with photos of many children, grandchildren, and great-grandchildren. When she knew certain people were coming to visit, she replaced all the pictures with their photos.

Teta Camilia was witty. It is difficult to recall a phone conversation when she did not make me laugh. With her great sense of humor, she often indulged in poking fun at members of her own family. I am sure many enjoyed the various anecdotes she told about me. But we all knew Teta Camilia loved us, that she prayed for us daily. She rejoiced at our good news and showed compassion when it was bad. She took great care in honoring big milestones from birthdays to graduations and weddings.

She often cheered me up and reminded me to weigh the negatives and positives when facing a difficult situation. Although we were not close geographically, Teta Camilia was near in my heart. And just one phone call away.

She loved life. She embraced it with the

fervor of youth. In particular, Teta Camilia enjoyed eating out. The last time I visited her in Bakersfield, California, we drove to her favorite breakfast restaurant. She insisted that she was inviting. With this she was always quite stubborn, and it was difficult to argue. She had a grand presence, and all the waitresses knew her well, treating her as a family member. It was a memorable breakfast.

Teta Camilia loved going to Vegas to play the slot machines, and my uncles indulged her with many trips. Invariably she would lose and promise never to go back, only to be first in the car at the next mention of a Vegas trip.

She challenged the best of us at card games and backgammon. It was no secret that she cheated sometimes, but that only seemed to be a problem if caught. While playing, her voice would occasionally rise, intensifying the pure delight of competing against her.

Teta Camilia passed away on August 5th, 2005. As the temperature in Bakersfield ascended to one hundred and two degrees Fahrenheit, my grandmother was climbing to heaven. But she left something behind, an aura of love. A love she unconditionally offered to God. A love she graciously bestowed on her family and everyone else who came her way. A love she nurtured through the life that was granted to her.

With your blessings Teta Camilia, and until we meet again, I pledge to continue your legacy of prayer, laughter, and love.

Thank you for the memories.

Thank you for being you.

Camilia Feghali and Nayef Feghali in Columbia, South
Carolina. 1992. Author's personal collection.

Toasting My Dad

December 12, 2006

I would like to present a toast to Bechara Feghali, the most honorable, generous, and loving man I have known. He was not a high-ranking official nor did he descend from noble blood, but he was my father.

In his twenties, he dutifully worked to provide for his younger siblings after his father passed at a young age. My dad was not a rich man, but throughout his life, he continued to support his mother and often bailed his siblings out of financial troubles.

In his thirties, he became a faithful husband to my mother and a loving father to the four of us. I remember the great pride he took when dressing us in our best outfits for Palm Sunday, decorating our tall white candles with Olive tree branches and white lilies, then processioning around church with the congregation.

In his forties, he struggled through the distant jungles of Africa and perspired under the hot sun of the Arab deserts, so that we could attend private schools.

"The children" were of paramount importance to my parents. Raising us was their primary obligation in life, regardless of any required sacrifices.

In his fifties, he faced the imminent failure of both kidneys, unemployment in a war-ridden country, and immigration to the United States. My father left everything behind to live in a land he had never visited, with new customs he couldn't explain, and a language he would never fully master. All this, so that my brothers and I could have a chance at a better future.

A kidney transplant allowed him to enjoy another twenty years of life. In the United

States, since my father could no longer work, the roles of my parents switched. But he remained a busy man and took his new responsibilities seriously. We always came home to cooked meals, the pantry was stocked, bills were paid, and the house was looked after. Dad chauffeured us to the University of South Carolina and work until we got our drivers licenses, he taught us how to drive, he bought our first cars, and he serviced them.

He breathed life into the front yard flowers so that they bloomed year-round. He grew a magnificent vegetable garden to which he tended judiciously, no matter the weather. Unfortunately, I did not inherit his green thumb; I somehow managed to kill whatever I planted. My father was a handy man, and everything had to be done the right way. Shortcuts were not an option.

In his sixties, he became a grandfather.

While I was recovering from childbirth, he stopped by my house three times a day with comforting home-cooked meals. I never expected a gentler role model. Dad lit up at the sight of his first grandson, and of course, Daniel worshipped his Jeddo. My father could repair anything from a broken bicycle, to a scout derby car, to an injured finger. "Jeddo fix it!" And he did.

He never knew his seventies. The kidney transplant was followed by an aorta transplant, a gallbladder operation, adult epilepsy, a broken hip, gout, cardiac stint, kidney dialysis, a spine bone transplant, until his body could take no more.

Dad was a walking testament of the miracles of modern medicine. We knew he was in a lot of pain, but he took it all in stride, never complaining, always thanking God for his blessings.

I remember rushing over to visit him on

the morning of his back surgery at Richland Memorial. My mother smiled as I walked in, while my dad reprimanded me for coming all the way to the hospital instead of heading straight into work. I was almost forty with children of my own, but he would never stop parenting me.

"Are you scared?" I asked.

"I'm never scared." He said, "I rely on God. His will shall prevail."

"I'm scared," I admitted.

"You have faith, you should not be."

My father never walked out of Richland Memorial. On December 2nd, 2003, God decided that Dad had carried his cross long enough.

It has been many years since that day, yet the loss still feels like it was only yesterday.

I miss you, Dad.

Here's to you and to the best memories a daughter could have!

Sylvie Feghali Smith and Bechara Feghali in Bsous,
Lebanon. 1965. Author's personal collection.

My Mother

May 3, 2007

My mother is wonderful.

"I wish I had your mom," my friends would say.

I could not help but wonder why they thought this, as I hid under the bed in an effort to avoid a beating.

My mother was strict. She overloaded me with chores while my three younger brothers, by virtue of being male, easily escaped the housework.

"How long do you think you can stay under there?" she snapped. "You're bound to come out at some point. Think you're clever, huh? I was a little girl once … "

Come to find out, the apple does not fall far from the tree.

Samia Feghali was born in the forties into a conservative, Catholic family in Lebanon. This was an era when girls rarely studied past middle school. She was not allowed to date, and she was not allowed to voice her opinion.

Samia was trained by her mother to be a mother. She was to live at home until she married, at which time she would move away from her parents' to live in her husband's home.

As a child, she was not a docile little girl. On the contrary, my mother was quite the rebel, preferring to risk punishment than to comply. She understood that fun had a price, and she was willing to pay for it.

In Samia's youth, one could imagine my grandmother running down the street to scold her because of some mischief. And my mother knew the consequences that awaited her, so she fled to her grandparents' yard.

Her escape came in the form of a tall fig tree. With the agility of a monkey, she would climb all the way to the top and start singing. Her grandfather, hearing the commotion, would come out and threaten to cut the tree. But Samia knew better than to come down right away. In time, her mother would catch her breath and calm down enough to lessen the repercussions.

It was customary in Lebanon to offer guests Turkish coffee. Served in small porcelain cups with frail handles that would often break, daughters were taught to reserve the nicer set for visitors.

One day, several church ladies came to the house for a get together. Samia wanted to play instead of accommodating them with food and drinks. When she emerged into the living room with a tray of shattered cups and dripping coffee, she was quick to find herself at the top of that fig tree.

My mother had amazing self-confidence. She was never deterred by the negative opinions of others, and Lebanese people tend to be quite judgmental.

When I was little, she would walk to the bakery to buy the staple pita bread, which came in loaves at least three times larger than the ones found in American grocery stores. Samia would carry the bag of bread on her head throughout the streets of Beirut to practice her balance. Everyone thought she was crazy, and to be honest, I didn't blame them. But Mom did not care. She thought it was good physical exercise, and that was that.

I can never forget stopping by Mom's house one evening with my sons, and finding her in bed with a scarf covering her hair. She insisted she was fine, but had a tough time explaining the scarf. Imagine our surprise when it slipped revealing bright orange hair. We didn't know whether to cry or laugh. Opting for the latter, we attempted to maintain our composure as she explained how she used "black" henna to strengthen her beautiful but thinning grey hair. To her horror, everything turned orange. "It was supposed to be black!" she lamented.

The situation was ironic given that just an hour prior, I had dragged my sons to the store to purchase hair color for myself. They really did not want to go, and amid their protests, tried to convince me I didn't need it, "You should let your hair go grey Mom, just like grandma's. Her hair is so pretty."

Not one to let the simple matter of flamboyant hair deter her, Samia took advantage of Thanksgiving that year to inform anyone who would listen that her pumpkin colored hair was a testament of her dedication to the Pilgrims' feast and the customs of her new country. It is just like my mother to turn an unfortunate situation into a reason to smile.

My mother was forbidden to pursue higher education because "a woman should not be more educated than her husband."

Nonetheless, she was always eager to learn. In the eighties, Lebanon was in the midst of war, and as a result, electricity, water, and food were rationed to one hour or two hours per day. This was the time when my mother first discovered and developed an interest in solar energy. As a science advocate, she was compelled to buy a solar water heating system for our home. "Now we will always have hot water," she announced proudly.

Alas she overlooked that, being in an active war zone, a young man endangered his life to install those solar panels, and they would likely be hit by a bomb the next day. The fact that we were renting the property and probably had no right installing such equipment did not stop her either.

We were one of the first to own a solar powered water heating system in the entire city of Beirut. If only we could have had running water to heat up, life would have been good.

Whatever you do, do not ask my mother for directions. If you are desperate, add an extra hour to her estimated travel time. If she offers to ride along to guide you, be wary. Be extremely wary.

On one occasion, Samia and I were very lost, but she insisted that she knew the way. I was driving, and my mother started navigating. Arriving at a crossroad, she motioned to the right with her hand and mumbled, "left, left."

I followed her gestures and turned right. The next twenty minutes were spent trying to get back on track, with my mom contending she had said left. What a stressful ride!

Mom is a fantastic chef. Everyone loves her home-cooked meals: kibbeh, mloukhiyi, mjaddara, fattoush, hummus, baklava … If you ask her for recipes, she will gladly give them to you. She will even type them up and email them, now that she has learned to use the computer.

When replicating her dish, however, do not be surprised if it comes out totally different.

My mother does not measure. She puts a little bit of this, more of that, a dash of this, and a sprinkle of that. So I strongly recommend that you leave the cooking to her and just come on over to enjoy the meal.

I have been blessed with a wonderful mother. When my brothers and I became parents, we learned to appreciate her unconditional love, her tremendous sacrifices, her terrible directions, her delicious cooking, and yes, even her occasional punishments.

Samia raised four responsible adults, and now at the age of sixty-two, has enrolled at University of South Carolina to continue her education and perhaps earn the degree she was always eager to get.

My aspiration is to be half as good a parent.

I love you, Mom!

Sylvie Feghali Smith and Samia Feghali in Blythewood, South Carolina. 2019. Author's personal collection.

Epilogue

October 25, 2019

We were never promised an easy, carefree visit to this world, and I am no different. I also had to learn how to navigate the highs and lows of life. Sometimes, a person dives to the bottom and climbing back up alone seems impossible. It is during these times that a support circle determines whether one sinks or swims.

I have been blessed with an incredible circle of people. My mother and father are my heroes. They did not tell my brothers and me how we should live our life, they taught by example, through their daily actions and decisions. They were selfless, brave, fair, and compassionate. My parents may not have agreed with some of my choices, but they nonetheless supported me unconditionally, and for that I am forever grateful.

How fortunate I am to have had my parents and grandparents as role models. They demonstrated what is most important in life: a strong faith, taking responsibility, and never giving up. I hope to have passed down their lessons to my children and perhaps one day to my grandchildren.

My three brothers and I have gone through quite a bit together. Though we currently live in different parts of the country, we continue to operate as a unit. Their wonderful wives, now my close sisters, have become active participants in my circle as well. These women have shown me they have my back no matter what.

Raising my sons as a single mom was not easy. Memories of hardships may rob me of my smile, but guiding Daniel and Michael through adulthood remains my most fulfilling accomplishment. These two boys were and are my greatest trials, my greatest loves, and they have enriched my life beyond measure. Seeing how they have grown into responsible, smart, capable young men with big hearts always brings my smile back. I am proud to be their mother.

Saving the best for last, I would like to acknowledge my dear husband, Tucker Smith. Without a doubt, he is my rock and the reason I am standing strong today. He is loving, wise, calm and witty, a credit to his wonderful parents who taught him high morals. Tucker has offered my children his unconditional support despite being their stepfather. No matter how rough the day might be, I am anchored in the knowledge that he will provide me a safe harbor. Life with my husband is both effortless and exciting. He encourages me to be the best version of myself, and for that, will always be the keeper of my heart.

Daniel Haddad, Tucker Smith, Sylvie Feghali Smith, and Michael Haddad in Blythewood, South Carolina. 2019. Author's personal collection.